**DOVER 3D Coloring**

# Christmas
## DESIGNS

# DOVER 3D Coloring Christmas DESIGNS

## MARTY NOBLE
## &
## JESSICA MAZURKIEWICZ

3-D GLASSES INSIDE!

## DOVER PUBLICATIONS, INC.
### MINEOLA, NEW YORK

# Note

Color some Christmas cheer with full-page patterns and mandalas created from traditional yuletide imagery, such as gingerbread men, reindeer, candles, ornaments, birds, stockings and more. Use crayons, marker, or colored pencils to add your own festive touch to the holidays.

*Copyright*

Copyright © 2009, 2013 by Dover Publications, Inc.
All rights reserved.

*Bibliographical Note*

This Dover edition, first published in 2013, contains all of the art from *Christmas Mandalas* by Marty Noble (pages 1-31, 63-92), published by Dover Publications, Inc., in 2013 and *ChristmasScapes* by Jessica Mazurkiewicz (pages 32-61, 93-122), published by Dover Publications, Inc., in 2009. One additional plate by Marty Noble is included in this edition.

*International Standard Book Number*
*ISBN-13: 978-0-486-49343-5*
*ISBN-10: 0-486-49343-1*

Manufactured in the United States by Courier Corporation
49343102    2013
www.doverpublications.com

1

10

14

17

Christmas Greetings

32

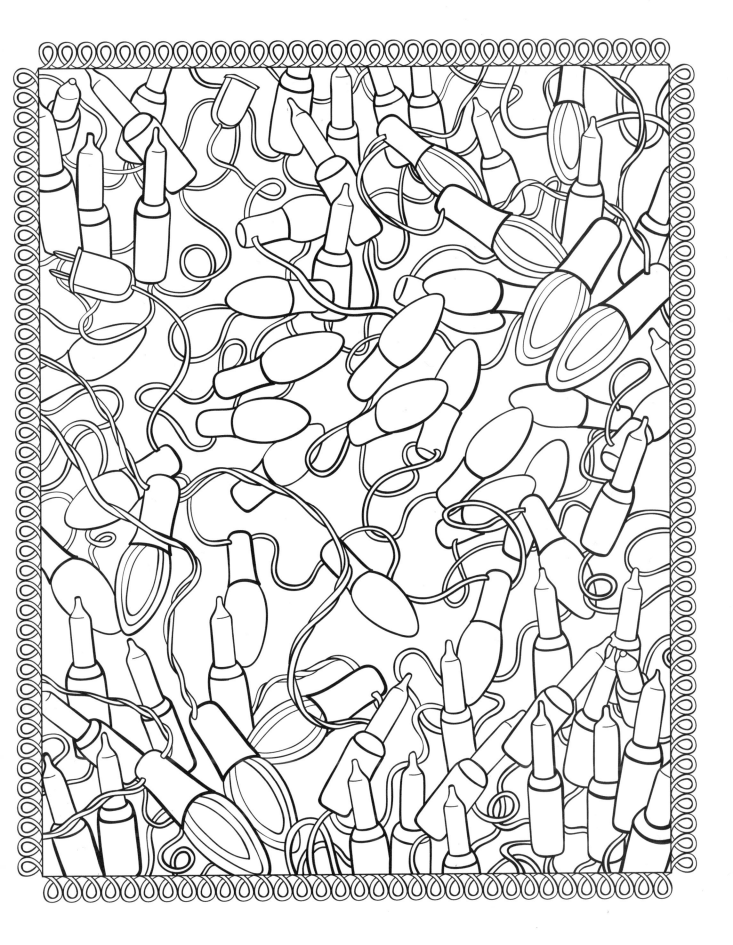

49

50

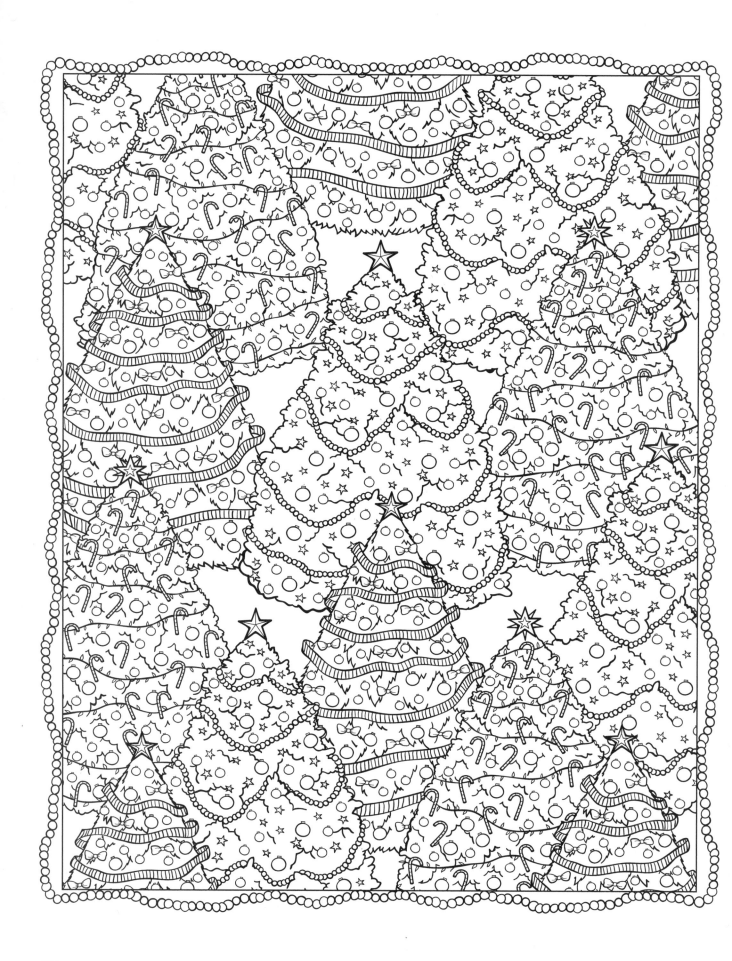

53

54

58

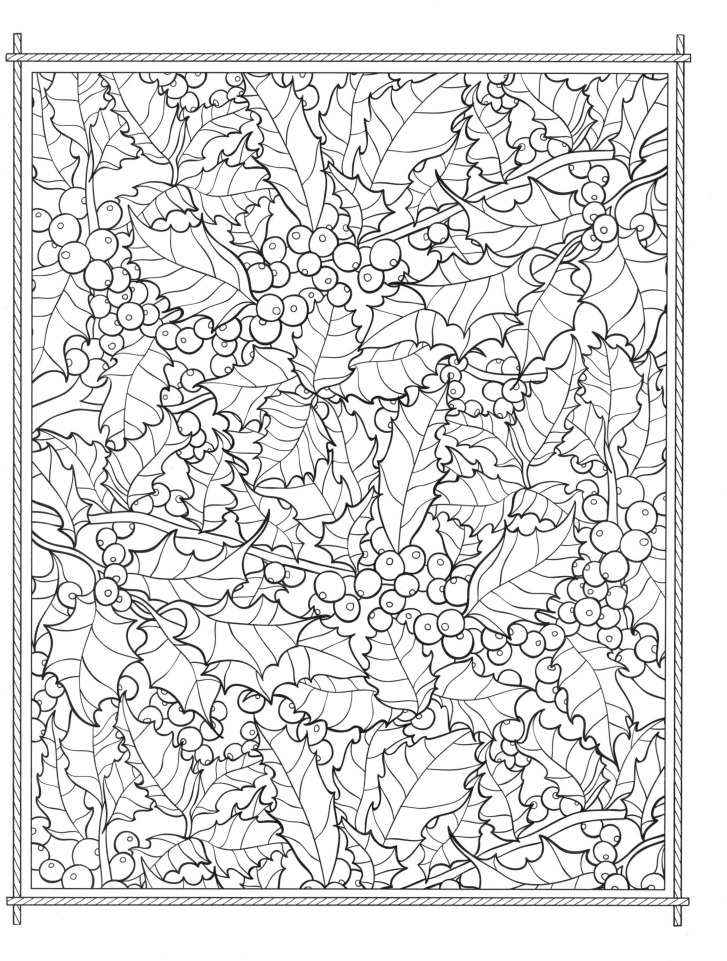

Christmas Greetings

95

96

101

103

104

111

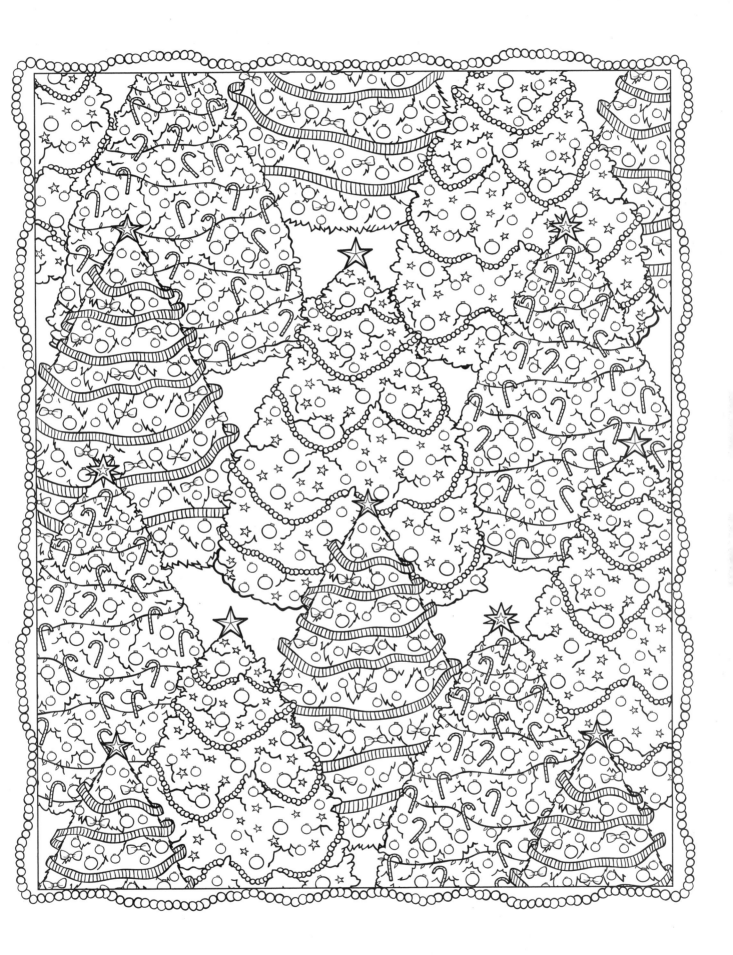

113

114

115

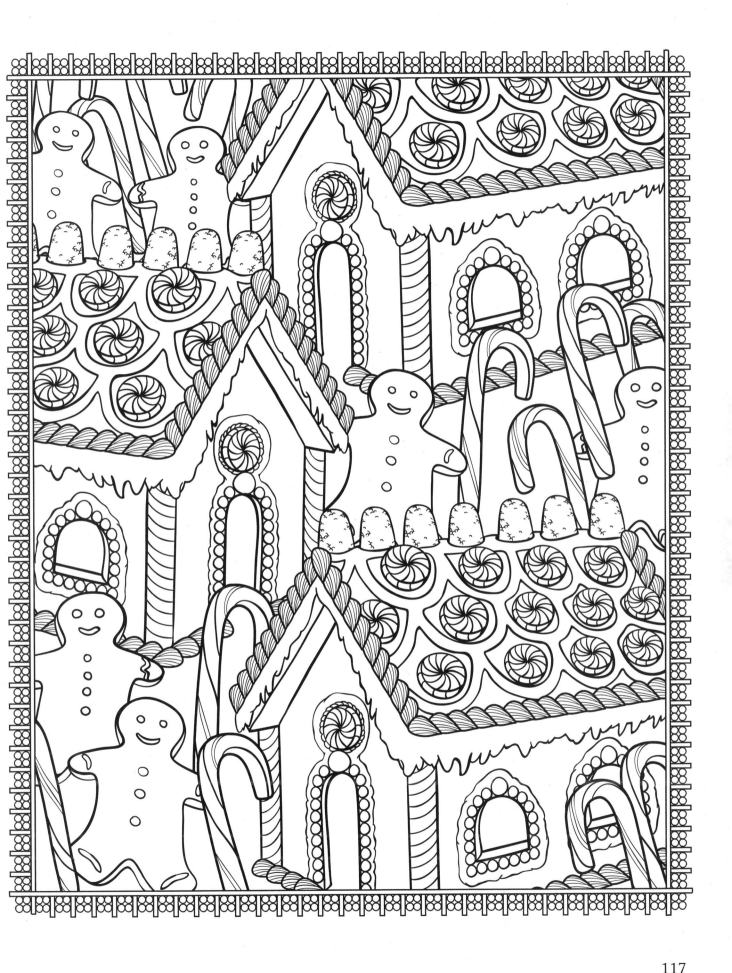

119

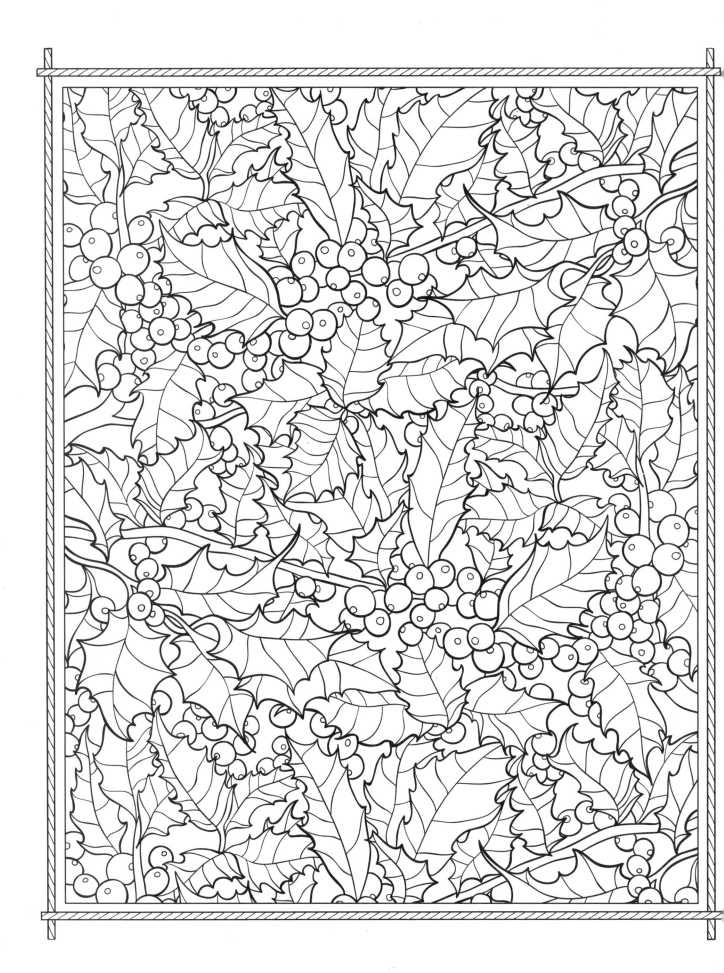